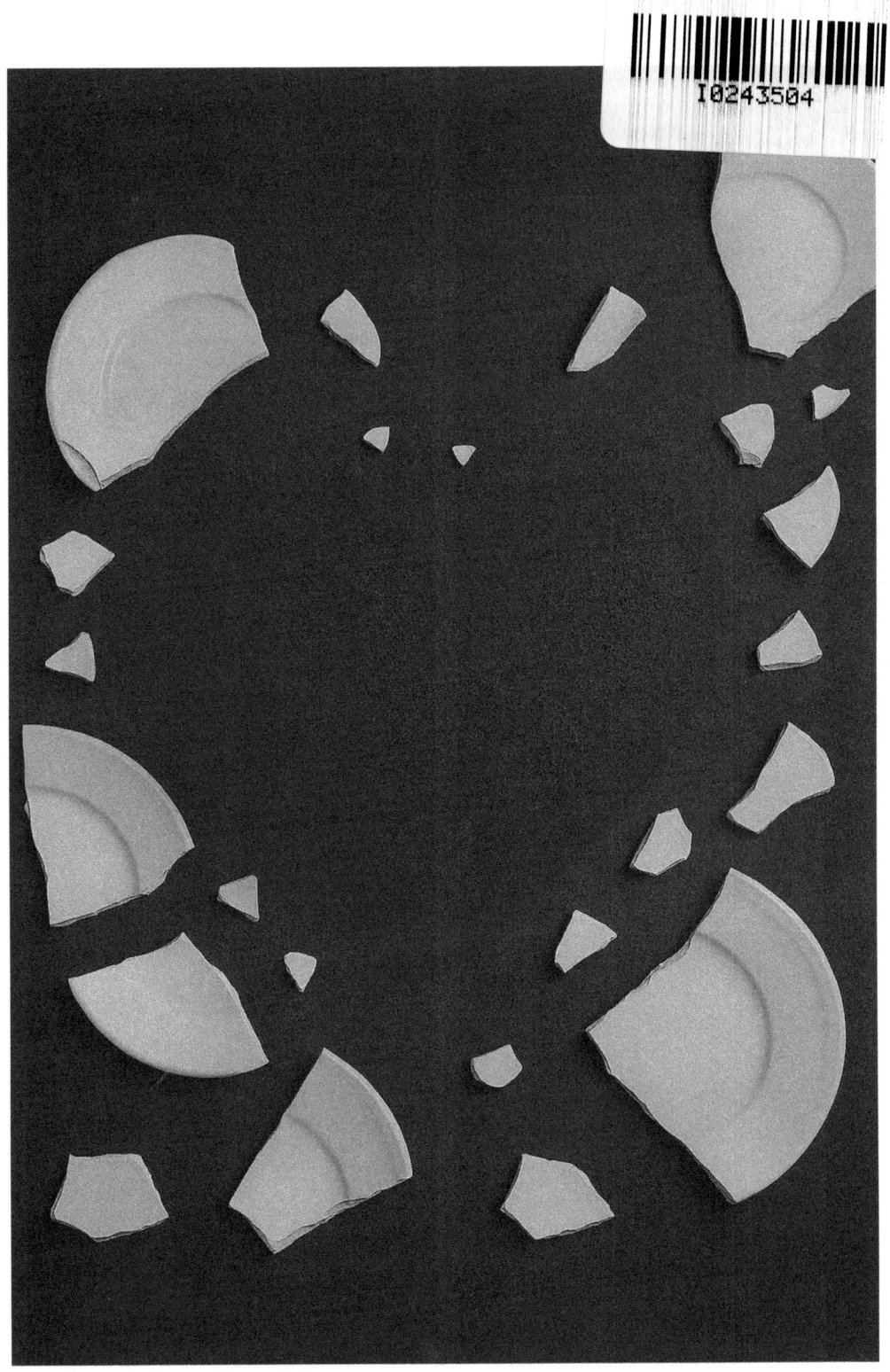

Not Easily Broken: 90 Days of Raw Healing

WorkBook Edition

© 2025 Tiffany A. Morgan

All Rights Reserved.

No part of this book may be reproduced, distributed, or transmitted in any form or by any means — including photocopying, recording, or any digital method without prior written permission of the author.

This book is a creative, educational, and reflective tool.

It is not a substitute for professional mental health, medical, or legal advice.

Readers are encouraged to seek appropriate professional support for personal needs.

For permissions and inquiries, contact:

Author: Tiffany A. Morgan

Cover Design: Tiffany Morgan

Interior Layout: Tiffany Morgan

ISBN: 979-8-9940577-3-5

Printed in the United States of America.

www.noteasilybrokenTm.com

Not Easily Broken: 90 Days of Raw Healing

If this book is in your hands, you have already done something brave.

You survived what tried to break you, and you are still here, still reaching for something better, even if your hands are shaking while you do it.

This workbook is not about pretty healing. It is not about pretending everything is fine, repeating cute quotes, and skipping past the parts that hurt. This is about raw healing, the kind that tells the truth. The kind that looks at the wounds, names what happened, and slowly begins to loosen the grip of shame, confusion and trauma.

You may be here because of a relationship that twisted your mind and heart.

You may be here because of narcissistic abuse, domestic violence, childhood trauma, or years of loving people who could not love you in a healthy way.

You may be here because you are tired of feeling crazy, tired of begging to be seen, tired of shrinking yourself just to keep the peace.

This workbook was written for you.

For the next 90 days, we will walk through layers of your story. Not to relive the pain, but to finally understand it, honor it, and begin to release it. You will see pieces of my story woven through these pages, not to center me, but to remind you that you are not alone and you are not imagining what you went through.

Inside you will find

- Full page lessons that break down trauma, survival responses, trauma bonds, and narcissistic patterns in simple language with real life examples
- Reflections on empathy and why people like you, with soft hearts and strong spirits, often attract and stay with people who harm them
- Journal prompts that ask hard questions and invite honest answers

- Affirmations that are not just cute words, but grounded declarations that speak directly to your nervous system and your inner child

- Rituals and practices for the mind, body, and spirit that can fit any belief system, whether you identify as spiritual, religious, or simply human and healing

- Information pulled from research and psychological studies so you can understand what happened to you on a brain and body level, not just an emotional level

- Practical tools for boundaries, emotional regulation, pattern recognition, and reclaiming your voice

These 90 days are not about becoming a perfect version of yourself. They are about becoming an honest version of yourself. A self who no longer carries the full weight of blame for what was done to you. A self who learns to hear their own voice again.

Some days will feel heavy. Some prompts may stir memories or emotions you have tucked away. That is normal. Go gently. Pause when you need to. Come back when you are ready. This is not a race. You are not behind. There is no wrong way to move through this workbook. The fact that you choose to keep turning pages is the work.

You may cry. You may get angry. You may feel numb sometimes. All of that is part of awakening after long term hurt. If at any point you feel overwhelmed or unsafe, please reach out to a trusted friend, mentor, support group, or trauma informed therapist. This workbook is a companion, not a replacement for professional help.

As you move through each phase, you will be invited to

- Name what really happened

- Understand how it shaped the way you think, love, and react

- Grieve the versions of you that were silenced or sacrificed

- Reclaim your power, your boundaries, and your right to peace

- Build daily routines that support your healing instead of your pain

You are not broken beyond repair.

You are not too much.

You are not impossible to love.

You are a person who experienced real harm and is now choosing real healing.

These pages are for every part of you. The strong one. The tired one. The hopeful one. The angry one. The one who still secretly wonders if it really was that bad. Bring all of them here. They all have a place in this journey.

Take a deep breath.

You do not have to have it all figured out to begin.

You only have to take the next honest step.

Turn the page.

Your 90 days of raw healing start now.

May your days be lighter and your journey be unforgettable!

Tiffany Morgan

DEDICATION

For the women who survived what should have destroyed them.

For the ones who carried entire worlds on their backs.

For the ones who loved too deeply and were wounded for it.

For the ones who rebuilt themselves from pieces others left behind.

For the ones who never gave up on their own becoming.

This book is for you.

Your healing is proof that transformation is real.

Your glow is the evidence that survival was never the end of your story.

INTRODUCTION TO PHASE THREE

THE RECLAMATION (Glow Up)

There comes a moment in every healing journey when the hurt no longer owns you.

When the story shifts. When the pain stops leading the way.

When your reflection changes... not because your face is different, but because your spirit is finally visible again.

This is that moment.

Phase Three is the Reclamation phase.

Not the redemption or glow up the world talks about....

not new clothes, not aesthetics, not attention, not external validation.

This is a soul-level glow up.

The glow up that comes from:

- healed boundaries
- self-trust
- clarity
- confidence
- peace
- discernment
- joy
- self-love

- alignment
- identity
- power
- emotional intelligence

This is a glow up that cannot be faked…

the kind born from nights you cried,

truths you faced,

patterns you broke,

and the version of yourself you refused to abandon.

In this phase, you reclaim:

- your voice
- your body
- your standards
- your dreams
- your desires
- your sensuality
- your identity
- your confidence
- your femininity
- your inner power
- your joy
- your life

Reclamation means taking your energy back from every place it leaked,

your worth back from every person who mishandled it,

your love back from every situation that didn't honor it,

your identity back from everything trauma tried to rewrite.

This is where you rise.

This is where you realign your life,

your relationships,

your habits,

your boundaries,

your routines,

your goals,

your vision.

This is where the woman you are becoming steps forward unapologetically.

Not the wounded version.

Not the survival version.

Not the silenced version.

Not the abandoned version.

Not the tired version.

The evolved version.

The healed version.

The grounded version.

The powerful version.

The glowing version.

The reclaimed version.

This phase is bold, bright, emotional, spiritual, grounded, embodied, and beautifully transformative.

Welcome to The Reclamation.

The phase where you don't just heal,

you take your life back.

PHASE THREE: THE RECLAMATION (GLOW UP)

Rising whole, radiant, and powerful.

DAY 61

THE RETURN OF SELF-LOVE: SEEING YOURSELF THROUGH HEALED EYES

You spent years seeing yourself through the lens of broken relationships,

trauma,

betrayal,

abandonment,

and insecurity.

But there is a moment in healing when you start seeing yourself clearly.

Not as the wounded woman.

Not as the rejected woman.

Not as the unloved woman.

Not as the silenced woman.

Not as the survival version of yourself.

But as the woman you truly are.

Your eyes soften when you look in the mirror.

Your voice becomes kinder.

Your choices become bolder.

Your soul becomes louder.

Your energy becomes stronger.

You realize:

- You are beautiful.
- You are worthy.
- You are capable.
- You are enough.
- You are radiant.
- You are more than what happened to you.
- You are becoming someone you can finally love.

Self-love is not arrogance.

Self-love is coming home.

Quote:

"The glow up begins the moment you see yourself clearly."

Affirmation:

I love who I am becoming.

WORKSHEET + ROUTINE

WORKSHEET: My Self-Love Return

1. What do I appreciate about myself now?
2. What have I overcome that I am proud of?
3. What part of me is blooming?
4. What does self-love look like daily?
5. What compliments do I finally believe?
6. What truth empowers me today?

Your Answers;

SELF-LOVE ROUTINE: 5-MINUTE GLOW ROUTINE

- place hand on heart
- breathe deeply
- say three things you love about yourself
- stretch or roll your shoulders
- whisper "I deserve softness"

UNIVERSAL PRACTICE : "Mirror Glow"

Look into the mirror daily and say:

"You are worthy of everything you desire."

Feel it through your soul.

Who is more deserving?

JOURNAL + AFFIRMATIONS

JOURNAL PROMPTS

1. What does a self-loved version of me act like?
2. What decisions does she make?
3. What boundaries does she keep?

AFFIRMATIONS

- I love myself boldly.
- My self-love is protection.
- I glow from within.
- I honor my beauty and worth.

DAY 62

THE FEMININE RISE: RECONNECTING TO BEAUTY, SOFTNESS & POWER

Your trauma hardened you,

but your healing softens you back into yourself.

Your feminine energy returns when you feel:

- safe
- supported
- seen
- regulated
- aligned
- respected

The feminine rise is not about aesthetics.

It's about allowing:

- your softness
- your intuition
- your sensuality
- your warmth

- your nurturing energy
- your creativity
- your emotional intelligence
- your confidence
- your mystery
- your flow

You are stepping into a version of femininity that is:

- healed
- grounded
- empowered
- intentional
- magnetic
- self-trusting
- deeply intuitive

- You no longer shrink your beauty.
- You no longer fear being seen.
- You no longer hide your light.
- You no longer apologize for existing boldly.

Your glow is not for attention.

It is the result of freedom.

Quote:

"A healed woman glows differently."

Affirmation:

I rise in soft power and divine femininity.

WORKSHEET + PSYCHOLOGY

WORKSHEET: My Feminine Rebirth

1. What parts of my femininity felt unsafe before?
2. What makes my feminine energy feel alive?
3. How do I express softness without losing strength?
4. What beauty rituals nourish me?
5. What feminine traits am I reclaiming?
6. What does my feminine power look like?

Your Answers;

PSYCHOLOGY INSIGHT: FEMININE ENERGY + SAFETY

Your feminine expression returns when your nervous system shifts out of survival mode.

Safety unlocks softness.

UNIVERSAL PRACTICE: "Feminine Glow"

A slow moment of:

- lotion or oil on skin
- gentle touch
- soft deep breathing
- "I am safe to soften" whispered softl

JOURNAL + AFFIRMATIONS

JOURNAL PROMPTS

1. How do I express my femininity freely now?
2. What does being seen feel like?
3. How do I honor my softness?

AFFIRMATIONS

- My feminine energy is powerful.
- I glow in softness and strength.
- I embrace beauty from within.
- My presence is radiant.

DAY 63

THE CONFIDENCE RENEWAL: WALKING WITH HEALED ENERGY

Confidence after trauma hits differently.

It isn't loud.

It isn't performative.

It isn't ego-driven.

It is rooted.

It is calm.

It is grounded.

It is steady.

It is unshakable because it comes from truth.

Your confidence returns when you realize:

you survived what was meant to destroy you

you learned yourself deeply

you trust your intuition

you understand your worth

you honor your boundaries

you no longer chase

you no longer beg

you no longer shrink

you no longer explain your value

Your confidence will not be everyone's favorite thing about you—

and that is okay.

Confidence exposes insecure people

and empowers the healed ones.

You don't need validation.

You don't need permission.

You walk differently when you know who you are.

Quote:

"Confidence is quiet. Alignment is loud."

Affirmation:

I walk in undeniable confidence.

WORKSHEET + BELIEF SHIFT

WORKSHEET: My Confidence Rebuild

1. What am I confident about now?
2. What lies did trauma tell me about myself?
3. What truth replaces those lies?
4. What behaviors reflect confidence in me?
5. What environments elevate my confidence?
6. What version of me stands tall?

Your Answers;

BELIEF SHIFT EXERCISE

Write:

"I release the belief that I am not enough."

Then rewrite:

"I am more than enough."

_____
_____
_____
_____
_____
_____
_____
_____
_____

UNIVERSAL PRACTICE: "Walk With Power"

Stand tall.

Roll your shoulders back.

Take one slow, intentional step forward.

Say:

"This is who I am now."

JOURNAL + AFFIRMATIONS

JOURNAL PROMPTS

1. When do I feel most confident?
2. What triggers my insecurity—and why?
3. How can I affirm myself daily?

AFFIRMATIONS

- My confidence is natural.
- I stand in my power.
- I radiate self-trust.
- I move with purpose.

DAY 64

BOUNDARIES AS ELEGANCE: THE ART OF GLOWING WHILE PROTECTING YOURSELF

When a healed woman sets boundaries,

it looks like elegance.

It looks like:

"No, thank you."

"I'm not available."

"That doesn't work for me."

"I'll think about it."

"I prefer something different."

"That's not aligned."

"I'm choosing peace."

Boundaries aren't aggression—

they're refinement.

You're learning to protect yourself without:

- explaining
- arguing
- defending
- pleasing
- over-giving
- performing
- shrinking
- self-betraying

Your glow becomes effortless when your boundaries are firm.

Boundaries are beauty.

Boundaries are confidence.

Boundaries are emotional luxury.

Quote:

"Elegance is the energy of a woman who protects her peace."

Affirmation:

My boundaries are a form of self-respect and grace.

WORKSHEET + PRACTICE

WORKSHEET: Elegant Boundary Setting

1. What boundary do I need most right now?
2. What makes boundary-setting hard?
3. What boundary protects my glow?
4. What does my body feel when I enforce boundaries?
5. What situations require stronger limits?
6. What elegant boundary phrase can I practice today?

Your Answers;

PRACTICE: ELEGANT BOUNDARY PHRASES

- "I'm unavailable for that."
- "That doesn't align with me."
- "Thank you, but no."
- "I need space from this conversation."

UNIVERSAL PRACTICE: "The Grace Line"

Close your eyes and whisper:

"My peace is sacred."

JOURNAL + AFFIRMATIONS

JOURNAL PROMPTS

1. What boundary did I wish I had earlier in life?
2. How do my boundaries reflect my growth?
3. Where can I practice elegant boundaries next?

AFFIRMATIONS

- My peace is luxury.
- My limits are respected.
- I protect myself with grace.
- I glow with boundaries.

DAY 65

THE BEAUTY OF BECOMING: EMBRACING WHO YOU ARE NOW

You are not who you were at the beginning of this workbook.

You have changed.

You have risen.

You have healed.

You have faced your shadows.

You have rebuilt your identity.

You have reclaimed your power.

You have softened and strengthened at the same time.

Becoming isn't about perfection.

It's about alignment.

You are becoming:

- clearer
- calmer
- sharper
- kinder

- braver
- wiser
- more intuitive
- more discerning
- more grounded
- more loving
- more confident

This is the glow up:

not external, but internal.

Your becoming is the most beautiful thing about you.

Quote:

"Becoming is the art of returning to yourself."

Affirmation:

I embrace who I am and who I am becoming.

WORKSHEET + IDENTITY

WORKSHEET: My Becoming

1. What am I most proud of in my healing?
2. What no longer fits the woman I'm becoming?
3. What habits support my evolution?
4. What emotions feel easier now?
5. What dreams feel possible again?
6. What identity am I stepping into fully?

Your Answers;

IDENTITY ALIGNMENT EXERCISE

Write a list titled:

"The Woman I Am Becoming."

Fill it with traits, habits, choices, and energy you want to embody.

_____
_____
_____
_____
_____
_____
_____
_____
_____
_____
_____
_____
_____
_____
_____
_____

UNIVERSAL PRACTICE: "The Becoming Breath"

Say softly:

"I am evolving beautifully."

JOURNAL + AFFIRMATIONS

JOURNAL PROMPTS

1. What does my healed identity feel like?
2. What am I ready to embody fully?
3. What version of me rises next?

AFFIRMATIONS

- I evolve with love.
- Becoming is my birthright.
- I honor my transformation.
- I glow from within.

DAY 66

THE SOFT LIFE WITH STANDARDS: PEACE THAT YOU EARNED

The soft life is not laziness.

It is not delusion.

It is not a trend.

The soft life is the lifestyle of someone who survived chaos

and finally chooses peace.

It means:

- you no longer argue
- you no longer chase
- you no longer force
- you no longer beg
- you no longer overgive
- you no longer shrink
- you no longer tolerate confusion
- you no longer excuse disrespect

It means you choose:

- ease
- rest
- beauty
- joy
- pleasure
- self-respect
- comfort
- alignment
- emotional safety
- soft routines
- healthy love
- healthy friendships
- healthy boundaries

Your softness is earned.

It is not careless...

it is intentional.

It is softness with standards.

Softness with boundaries.

Softness with discernment.

Softness supported by strength.

This level of soft living comes from survival, healing, and wisdom.

You deserve a life that feels gentle.

You deserve a life that feels peaceful.

You deserve softness that doesn't ask you to suffer first.

Quote:

"Soft life doesn't mean weak. It means you healed enough to stop choosing struggle."

Affirmation:

I choose a soft life that honors my healing and my standards.

WORKSHEET + PSYCHOLOGY

WORKSHEET: Building My Soft Life

1. What habits create softness for me?
2. What makes my life feel chaotic?
3. What standard protects my peace?
4. What does a soft day look like?
5. Where do I need more rest?
6. What soft boundary will I set?

Your Answers;

PSYCHOLOGY INSIGHT: SOFTNESS & NERVOUS SYSTEM SAFETY

Soft living calms the sympathetic nervous system,

reducing cortisol and strengthening emotional resilience.

Softness heals the body just as much as the mind.

UNIVERSAL PRACTICE: "The Soft Breath"

Inhale: "I soften."

Exhale: "I am safe."

JOURNAL + AFFIRMATIONS

JOURNAL PROMPTS

1. What does softness look like for me personally?
2. What emotional labor am I no longer willing to carry?
3. How can I make softness my new normal?

AFFIRMATIONS

- Softness is my strength.
- Peace is my lifestyle.
- I choose ease and alignment.
- My softness is protected.

DAY 67

THE EMBODIED GLOW: HEALING YOUR RELATIONSHIP WITH YOUR BODY

Your body was once a battleground.

A place that held trauma.

A place that carried pain.

A place that felt unsafe.

A place you may have disconnected from to survive.

But now, you are coming home to your body.

Not for looks.

Not for validation.

Not for comparison.

But because your body is your first home

and she deserves love, safety, tenderness, and presence.

Your embodied glow comes from:

- gentle movement

- hydration
- rest
- touch that feels safe
- affirming your beauty
- caring for your skin
- nourishing foods
- stretching
- breathing deeply
- choosing clothes that feel comfortable
- honoring your sensuality
- releasing shame
- reconnecting with pleasure

This is body reclamation.

Not perfection.

Not performance.

Not weight.

Not aesthetics.

This is you becoming present in your body again.

Quote:

"Your body is not a project. It is a home."

Affirmation:

My body is sacred, beautiful, and worthy of gentle care.

WORKSHEET + SOMATIC WORK

WORKSHEET: Reclaiming My Body

1. What part of my body have I disconnected from?
2. What messages did trauma teach me about my body?
3. What truth do I want my body to hear now?
4. What physical practices feel good to me?
5. What does body safety feel like?
6. How can I care for my body today?

Your Answers;

SOMATIC HEALING: EMBODIMENT PRACTICE

- breathe into your belly
- stretch your shoulders and chest
- roll your hips slowly
- place hands gently over your heart
- acknowledge:

"This is my home."

UNIVERSAL PRACTICE: "Skin Gratitude"

Apply lotion or oil gently, saying:

"Thank you for carrying me through everything."

JOURNAL + AFFIRMATIONS

JOURNAL PROMPTS

1. What do I appreciate about my body now?
2. Where did I abandon my body, and how do I return?
3. What new relationship do I want with my body

AFFIRMATIONS

- I live in my body with love.
- My body is worthy of tenderness.
- I honor this vessel that survived for me.
- My glow begins within.

DAY 68

YOUR MAGNETIC ENERGY: ATTRACTING FROM HEALING, NOT WOUNDS

There is a shift in the way you attract people when you heal.

Before healing, you attracted:

- people who fed on your empathy
- people who exploited your softness
- people who mirrored your wounds
- people who manipulated your kindness
- people who loved your brokenness
- people who benefitted from your silence

But when you heal?

Your energy changes.

Your presence changes.

Your aura changes.

Your standards change.

Your boundaries change.

Your intuition changes.

Your healed aura attracts:

- people who value you
- people who support you
- people who speak truth
- people who give consistently
- people who honor boundaries
- people who love safely
- people who bring peace
- people who match your energy

Your glow is not just beauty…

it is emotional clarity.

And clarity is magnetic.

Quote:

"When your energy shifts, your entire life recalibrates."

Affirmation:

I attract what aligns with my healed self.

WORKSHEET + PSYCHOLOGY

WORKSHEET: My Magnetic Energy Shift

1. What energy did I give off before healing?
2. What kind of people did that attract?
3. What energy do I embody now?
4. What kind of relationships does that invite?
5. What energy am I no longer available for?
6. What aligns with my glow?

Your Answers;

PSYCHOLOGY INSIGHT: ENERGY & ATTRACTION PATTERNS

Humans are drawn to familiar dynamics.

When your inner world heals,

your outer world must rearrange.

It is psychology.

It is biology.

It is spiritual alignment.

UNIVERSAL PRACTICE: "The Energy Recalibration"

Stand still.

Imagine a golden light around you.

Say softly:

"Only what aligns can enter my space."

JOURNAL + AFFIRMATIONS

JOURNAL PROMPTS

1. What qualities do I now attract?
2. What relationships no longer match my energy?
3. What energy am I stepping into fully?

AFFIRMATIONS

- My energy is powerful.
- I attract alignment with ease.
- My glow draws what is meant for me.
- I radiate healed energy.

WITHOUT BECOMING ONE

Breaking the cycle without hardening your heart

DISCLAIMER + INTENTION PAGE

READ THIS BEFORE CONTINUING

This section is not about revenge... It is not about blame... It is not about reliving harm.

This section exists to protect your integrity.

Healing does not end when the danger is gone... Healing deepens when you are no longer reacting.

The purpose of this section is to help you:

- process anger without weaponizing it
- acknowledge pain without passing it on
- understand how trauma can distort behavior
- interrupt cycles before they repeat
- choose who you become after survival

This is not a judgment of victims but instead is an invitation to consciousness.

Pain explains behavior. It does not excuse harm.

Read this section slowly.
Honestly and with compassion for who you were and responsibility for who you are becoming.

HOW TO KILL A MONSTER

WITHOUT BECOMING ONE

The monster is gone.

The manipulation ended...

The betrayal was exposed...

The truth surfaced...

The threat stopped.

And now there is silence.

This is the part no one prepares you for. Once the monster is dead,

there is no enemy left to fight, only pain that needs somewhere to go.

This is where healing either matures or mutates.

If pain is not processed, it hardens...

If anger is not honored, it leaks...

If grief is not felt, it turns cold.

This is how survivors can unintentionally become harmful. Its not through cruelty, but through unhealed survival strategies.

THE TRUTH NO ONE LIKES TO SAY

Hurt people don't just hurt people accidentally.

Unhealed people can become harmful.

Betrayed people can become bitter.

Victims can become emotionally abusive.

Survivors can become controlling.

Wounded people can weaponize their pain.

Not because they are evil but because pain wants somewhere to live.

And if it isn't healed, it leaks.

WHEN SURVIVAL BECOMES IDENTITY

Trauma teaches the brain:

- Control equals safety

- Distance equals protection

- Softness equals danger

- Vulnerability equals loss

Without healing, survival skills become personality traits.

You may notice:

- emotional withdrawal

- distrust of everyone

- punishing silence

- hyper-independence

- preemptive rejection

- controlling behaviors

- emotional numbing

- bitterness disguised as boundaries

This is not strength.

This is armor that stayed on too long.

THE PSYCHOLOGY (WHY THIS HAPPENS)

Research shows:

• Survivors of betrayal trauma are significantly more likely to develop avoidant or controlling attachment patterns

• Nearly 40 percent of individuals who engage in emotionally abusive behaviors report being victims themselves

• Chronic trauma dysregulates the prefrontal cortex, impairing impulse control and emotional regulation

• Unprocessed anger increases the likelihood of reenactment, projection, and emotional retaliation

Trauma wires the brain for defense.

Healing rewires it for discernment.

THE STATISTICS (U.S. BASED)

• Studies show over 60% of people who experience childhood abuse struggle with emotional regulation in adulthood

• Survivors of betrayal trauma are 2–3x more likely to develop controlling or avoidant attachment patterns

• Nearly 40% of domestic violence perpetrators report being victims of abuse themselves

• Emotional abuse is most often unintentional and rooted in unhealed trauma

• Cycles continue not because people are cruel — but because pain was never taught how to stop

Trauma explains behavior.

It does not excuse it.

THE DIFFERENCE BETWEEN BOUNDARIES AND BITTERNESS

Boundaries sound like:

"I won't accept this."

"I need space."

"This doesn't feel safe for me."

"I choose differently now."

Bitterness sounds like:

"No one can be trusted."

"People always leave."

"I'll hurt them before they hurt me."

"I don't care anymore."

"Love isn't real."

Boundaries say:

"I will not tolerate this."

Bitterness says:

"No one deserves access to me."

Boundaries are calm.

Bitterness is reactive.

Boundaries protect peace.

Bitterness poisons it.

If your boundary requires cruelty to hold,

it is fear not clarity.

Boundaries protect.

Bitterness poisons.

HOW TO KILL THE MONSTER WITHOUT BECOMING IT

You don't kill the monster by hardening.

You kill it by interrupting the cycle.

HOW THE MONSTER ACTUALLY DIES

Not by vengeance.

Not by coldness.

Not by becoming unreachable.

The monster dies when:

- you feel anger without acting it out

- you choose truth over punishment

- you hold boundaries without cruelty

- you speak pain without using it as a weapon

- you stop proving strength through detachment

- you choose growth over control

The cycle ends when consciousness begins. The monster doesn't die when you become ruthless. It dies when you become self-aware.

WORKSHEET: CHECKING MY SHADOW

1. How has my pain changed the way I treat others?

2. What behaviors do I justify as "protection" that might actually be fear?

3. Where do I withhold love, communication, or softness as punishment?

4. What am I afraid would happen if I stayed open but boundaried?

5. What parts of my pain need healing and not guarding?

6. What version of myself am I committed to becoming?

JOURNAL PROMPTS

1. When did I first notice bitterness trying to take root?

2. What would healing look like instead of hardening?

3. How do I hold my pain without passing it on?

4. What patterns do I refuse to repeat?

5. Who do I want to be after the betrayal — not because of it?

A NOTE TO THE SELF

I see how angry you were.

I see how much it hurt.

I see how easy it would have been to become cold.

But I choose healing.

I choose softness with boundaries.

I choose awareness over rage.

I choose integrity over bitterness.

I choose to break the cycle and not continue it.

AFFIRMATIONS

- My pain does not give me permission to harm.

- I can heal without becoming bitter.

- I release vengeance and choose growth.

- I break cycles by staying conscious.

- I am responsible for who I become.

- I kill the monster by refusing to carry it forward.

CLOSING TRUTH

The greatest victory is not surviving the monster.

It's not becoming one.

And choosing that path every day

is the bravest work you will ever do.

DAY 69

THE LUXURY OF EMOTIONAL STABILITY: YOUR NEW NORMAL

Stability is luxury when you come from chaos.

Not emotional numbness.

Not emotional distance.

Not emotional restriction.

But emotional stability.

Where:

- you don't lose yourself in someone
- you don't fear abandonment
- you don't chase attention
- you don't confuse intensity for love
- you don't internalize rejection
- you don't spiral from small triggers
- you don't accept disrespect
- you don't settle for half-love
- you don't choose chaos

Emotional stability is the final glow of healing.

It feels like:

- clarity
- neutrality
- slow reactions
- wise responses
- steady mood
- comfortable silence
- regulation
- certainty
- control over your emotions
- understanding your body
- having emotional space

Emotional stability makes you powerful...

unbothered, aligned, grounded, and selective.

Quote:

"Emotional stability is wealth."

Affirmation:

My emotions are steady, wise, and grounded.

WORKSHEET + PSYCHOLOGY

WORKSHEET: Building My Emotional Stability

1. What used to destabilize me?
2. What triggers do I manage better now?
3. What calms my emotions quickly?
4. What routine supports regulation?
5. What emotional boundaries protect me?
6. What stable habits define my new self?

Your Answers;

PSYCHOLOGY INSIGHT: EMOTIONAL REGULATION

Stability comes from:

- nervous system healing
- consistent routine
- healthy relationships
- strong intuition
- self-trust
- aligned boundaries

This is psychological growth and emotional elevation.

UNIVERSAL PRACTICE: "The Stability Seat"

Sit still for 1–2 minutes.

Feel your body supported beneath you.

Say:

"I am grounded."

JOURNAL + AFFIRMATIONS

JOURNAL PROMPTS

1. What emotional shifts am I proud of?
2. What does stability mean to me?
3. What stability practices can I deepen?

AFFIRMATIONS

- I am emotionally steady.
- Peace runs through me.
- I honor my stability daily.
- I am grounded and whole.

DAY 70

BECOMING "HER": THE MOST HEALED, POWERFUL VERSION OF YOU

Becoming HER means rising into the woman you always knew you could be.

She is not perfect…

she is aligned.

She is:

- glowing
- peaceful
- protected
- clear
- centered
- respected
- confident
- intentional
- loved
- loving
- wise

- disciplined
- soft
- strong
- magnetic
- whole

Becoming HER means:

- you listen to your intuition
- you honor your boundaries
- you speak your truth
- you choose yourself
- you pour into your body
- you embrace your femininity
- you practice self-love
- you walk in discernment
- you break generational patterns
- you build a life you don't need to escape
- you stop apologizing for existing
- you become the love you needed

You are not chasing HER.

You are unveiling HER.

Everything you need is already within you.

This phase simply reveals it.

Quote:

"Becoming HER is not a glow up. It is a return to your highest self."

Affirmation:

I am becoming HER every day.

WORKSHEET + IDENTITY

WORKSHEET: Becoming HER

1. What qualities define HER?

2. What habits does SHE live by?

3. What choices does SHE make?

4. What does SHE no longer tolerate?

5. What brings HER joy?

6. What step can I take today to become HER?

Your Answers;

IDENTITY PRACTICE: THE "HER LIST"

List 10 ways you are already HER

and 10 ways you are becoming HER.

UNIVERSAL PRACTICE: "HER Alignment"

Stand tall.

Lift your chin.

Say:

"I am stepping into HER now."

JOURNAL + AFFIRMATIONS

JOURNAL PROMPTS

1. What version of HER lives inside me?
2. What actions align me with HER?
3. What part of HER is emerging now?

AFFIRMATIONS

- I am HER.
- I rise into my highest self.
- I walk with grace and power.
- I embody my glow fully.

DAY 71

THE ART OF DETACHMENT: STAYING GROUNDED IN YOUR PEACE

Detachment is not coldness.

It is not indifference.

It is not a lack of emotion.

True detachment is emotional freedom.

Detachment means:

- you don't cling
- you don't chase
- you don't beg
- you don't over-explain
- you don't monitor their behavior
- you don't lose yourself in the outcome
- you don't internalize someone else's choices
- you don't force connections

Detachment is connection without desperation.

Care without self-abandonment.

Love without losing yourself.

Openness without overgiving.

Presence without attachment to outcome.

Detachment is:

- "I desire this, but I don't need it."
- "I care, but I won't abandon myself."
- "I love, but I won't lose my peace."
- "I am here, but I'm not tied to what isn't for me."

Detachment is alignment.

Detachment is emotional power.

Detachment is a glow.

Quote:

"When you detach, you stop bleeding for things that never deserved your sacrifice."

Affirmation:

I am connected but never controlled. I detach in peace.

WORKSHEET + PSYCHOLOGY

WORKSHEET: Practicing Healthy Detachment

1. Where do I attach too tightly?

2. What situations drain my energy?

3. What am I afraid to lose, and why?

4. What does healthy detachment mean to me?

5. What would I do differently if I detached emotionally?

6. How does detachment protect my peace?

Your Answers;

PSYCHOLOGY INSIGHT: ATTACHMENT + DETACHMENT

Detachment activates the logical mind and calms the emotional threat system.

It creates:

- clarity
- emotional distance
- stronger boundaries
- increased self-trust
- less anxiety
- more alignment

UNIVERSAL PRACTICE: "Release the Outcome"

Hold your hands out.

Visualize the situation.

Whisper:

"I release what is not mine to control."

JOURNAL + AFFIRMATIONS

JOURNAL PROMPTS

1. Where do I need more emotional space?
2. What outcome am I releasing?
3. How does detachment feel in my body?

AFFIRMATIONS

- I choose freedom over fear.
- Detachment protects my peace.
- I am grounded and centered.
- What is meant for me flows to me.

DAY 72

THE ELEVATED STANDARD: BECOMING UNAVAILABLE FOR ANYTHING LESS THAN PEACE

There comes a point in healing where your standards rise silently.

Not because you're picky.

Not because you're bitter.

Not because you're "too much."

But because you finally understand your worth.

Your elevated standard means:

- you don't entertain mixed signals
- you don't invest in confusion
- you don't stay where you're not valued
- you don't settle for half-effort
- you don't accept inconsistency
- you don't respond to disrespect
- you don't justify potential

- you don't cling to maybes
- you don't bargain with your peace

Your standard isn't punishment—

it's alignment.

You are no longer available for:

- low effort
- low integrity
- low accountability
- low empathy
- low emotional intelligence
- low energy men
- low vibrations
- low reciprocity

Your standard is not about being difficult.

Your standard is about being protected.

Quote:

"My standard is not negotiable—because my peace is not negotiable."

Affirmation:

I am unavailable for anything that costs me peace.

WORKSHEET + CLARITY WORK

WORKSHEET: My New Standard

1. What did I accept before healing?
2. What am I never accepting again?
3. What does my elevated standard require?
4. What does respect look like now?
5. What does emotional safety look like?
6. What aligns with the woman I am becoming?

Your Answers;

CLARITY EXERCISE: NON-NEGOTIABLES

Write three lists:

- My bare minimums
- My must-haves
- My deal-breakers

UNIVERSAL PRACTICE : "The Standard Stand"

Stand firmly.

Say:

"My standards protect my peace, and my peace is sacred."

JOURNAL + AFFIRMATIONS

JOURNAL PROMPTS

1. What new standards feel empowering?
2. What pattern am I breaking for good?
3. How will I uphold my standards moving forward?

AFFIRMATIONS

- My standards are high because my value is high.
- I protect my peace at all costs.
- I choose alignment over attachment.
- I honor my worth.

DAY 73

THE POWER OF CHOOSING YOURSELF FIRST

Choosing yourself first is not selfish.

It is self-preserving.

It is self-loving.

It is self-restoring.

You spent years choosing:

people before peace

relationships before sanity

needs of others before your own

apologies before accountability

hope before reality

their comfort before your boundaries

Choosing yourself first means:

- "I hear your need, but I will not abandon myself for it."
- "I matter, too."

- "My voice counts."
- "My rest is important."
- "My healing comes first."
- "My boundaries are law."

When you choose yourself first,

your whole life shifts.

You stop:

- over-giving
- over-apologizing
- over-explaining
- over-functioning
- over-caring
- over-investing

You start:

- thinking clearly
- loving intentionally
- setting boundaries
- protecting your inner world
- honoring your energy
- making aligned decisions

- trusting your instincts

You cannot pour into anyone if your cup is shattered.

Choosing yourself is choosing survival, healing, and joy.

Quote:

"When you choose yourself, everything that isn't aligned quietly falls away."

Affirmation:

I choose myself without guilt or hesitation.

WORKSHEET + ACT OF SELF

WORKSHEET: Putting Myself First

1. Where do I abandon myself most often?
2. What guilt shows up when I choose myself?
3. What truth can replace that guilt?
4. What decision honors me today?
5. What do I need right now emotionally?
6. What does choosing myself look like in action?

Your Answers;

ACT OF SELF: DAILY SELF-PRIORITY CHECK-IN

Ask yourself each morning:

"What do I need today?"

"How can I honor myself?"

"What boundary protects me?"

UNIVERSAL PRACTICE : "The Self-First Breath"

Hand on heart.

Whisper:

"I choose me first."

JOURNAL + AFFIRMATIONS

JOURNAL PROMPTS

1. Where do I struggle to choose myself?
2. What childhood wound taught me self-abandonment?
3. How does choosing myself change my life?

AFFIRMATIONS

- I choose myself with ease.
- My needs matter.
- I honor my emotional world.
- Self-priority is self-love.

DAY 74

THE SACRED NOURISHMENT: POURING INTO YOURSELF INTENTIONALLY

You deserve nourishment...

not just rest,

not just healing,

not just survival.

Real nourishment.

Nourishment is the act of feeding the parts of you that were starved:

your joy

your creativity

your sensuality

your spirit

your rest

your curiosity

your hobbies

your goals

your desires

your inner child

Nourishment looks like:

- long showers
- slow mornings
- full meals
- decorating your space
- reading books that inspire you
- stretching
- creating beauty
- writing
- laughing
- stepping outside
- hydrating
- journaling
- doing your hair or skincare
- learning new skills
- resting without guilt

Nourishment is not luxury...

it is maintenance.

Your glow requires nourishment,

not neglect.

Quote:

"*Nourish the parts of you that life once starved.*"

Affirmation:

I nourish myself with intention, love, and care.

WORKSHEET + PRACTICE

WORKSHEET: Nourishing My Inner World

1. What parts of my life feel depleted?
2. What nourishes my mind?
3. What nourishes my body?
4. What nourishes my spirit?
5. What nourishes my joy?
6. What nourishing habit can I build today?

Your Answers;

NOURISHMENT PRACTICE: THE "5 POURS"

Pour into yourself through:

1. Movement
2. Rest
3. Beauty
4. Creativity
5. Stillness

UNIVERSAL PRACTICE : "The Nourish Touch"

Place hands on your chest and stomach.

Whisper:

"I feed my soul."

JOURNAL + AFFIRMATIONS

JOURNAL PROMPTS

1. What do I need more of?
2. What drains me that I need less of?
3. How does nourishment change my glow?

AFFIRMATIONS

- I nourish my whole self.
- My glow comes from within.
- I honor my body and spirit.
- I pour into myself daily.

DAY 75

THE AUDACITY OF JOY: LETTING HAPPINESS IN WITHOUT FEAR

After trauma, joy can feel dangerous.

You fear:

- it won't last
- someone will ruin it
- you don't deserve it
- it's "too good to be true"
- something bad will follow
- you shouldn't feel this happy

But this fear is just a trauma response...

your brain learned to expect pain.

Healing teaches you that joy is not a trap.

Joy is not a threat.

Joy is not a weakness.

Joy is medicine.

Joy is resilience.

Joy is rebellion.

Joy is a return to life.

Joy is a declaration that pain did not win.

It is okay to smile again.

It is okay to laugh.

It is okay to trust moments of peace.

It is okay to let your heart feel light.

You deserve joy without bracing for impact.

Quote:

"Joy is your birthright, not a reward you must earn."

Affirmation:

I allow joy to enter my life freely and fully.

WORKSHEET + PSYCHOLOGY

WORKSHEET: Welcoming Joy Again

1. What scares me about happiness?
2. When did joy last feel safe?
3. What brings me genuine joy?
4. How can I let myself enjoy small moments?
5. What wounds block my joy?
6. What joyful experience can I welcome today?

Your Answers;

PSYCHOLOGY INSIGHT: JOY & TRAUMA

Trauma wires the brain to expect danger.

Healing rewires the brain to accept comfort and joy.

Joy is a nervous system repair tool.

UNIVERSAL PRACTICE: "The Joy Breath"

Smile gently.

Inhale: "I welcome joy."

Exhale: "I am safe to feel happy."

JOURNAL + AFFIRMATIONS

JOURNAL PROMPTS

1. What joy do I want to experience more often?
2. What belief keeps me from embracing joy?
3. How can I teach my body that joy is safe?

AFFIRMATIONS

- Joy is safe for me.
- Happiness belongs in my life.
- I welcome light into my heart.
- Joy is part of my healing.

BONUS INSERT II:

HAPPINESS: WHAT IT REALLY IS, WHY IT FEELS HARD, AND HOW TO CULTIVATE IT

Happiness is not a destination.

It is not constant.

It is not a mood you chase or a moment you stumble into.

Happiness is a practice.

A state of alignment.

The natural byproduct of a regulated nervous system, healed patterns, strong boundaries, and a life that honors your truth.

It is not found in another person.

It is not found in perfection.

It is not found in escape.

Happiness is:

clarity

peace

intention

presence

stability

self-honoring choices

emotional safety

connection

gratitude

freedom

purpose

Happiness grows from the inside out.

But for many survivors, happiness feels foreign —

not because you're incapable of it,

but because your nervous system was conditioned to prioritize survival over joy.

Let's explore why.

WHY HAPPINESS FEELS UNFAMILIAR FOR TRAUMA SURVIVORS

1. Your brain was trained to anticipate danger

Growing up in chaos or instability teaches your body to scan for threats, not joy.

Happiness feels unsafe because it's unfamiliar.

2. You learned to associate calm with the "calm before the storm"

Peace feels uncomfortable when you've lived in emotional turbulence.

3. You never saw modeled joy

If the adults around you were stressed, angry, or numb, you learned that happiness is rare or unrealistic.

4. You attached happiness to someone else's approval

Trauma teaches you to outsource joy instead of generate it internally.

5. You confuse happiness with productivity or perfection

Survivors often feel guilty resting or enjoying themselves.

6. Your nervous system equates joy with vulnerability

To feel happy is to feel open, and openness once equaled danger.

Happiness is not missing from your life...

your body simply hasn't learned to trust it yet.

WHAT HAPPINESS ACTUALLY IS

Happiness is not:

- excitement
- adrenaline
- perfection
- being busy
- high emotions
- constant positivity

Happiness is:

- Emotional stability
- A calm mind
- A regulated nervous system
- Being able to trust yourself
- Making aligned decisions
- Choosing environments that feed you
- Letting go of what drains you
- Knowing your worth
- Practicing gratitude
- Creating a life that matches your values

Happiness is steady, not loud.

Warm, not overwhelming.

A soft glow, not a blazing flame.

THE SCIENCE BEHIND HAPPINESS

Dopamine

Reward, motivation, anticipation of pleasure.

Serotonin

Mood stability, confidence, emotional grounding.

Oxytocin

Connection, bonding, safety.

Endorphins

Relief, comfort, relaxation.

Survivors often lack access to consistent serotonin and oxytocin due to chronic stress or trauma.

This makes happiness feel hard to access …

but absolutely possible to rebuild.

Happiness can be trained like a muscle.

HAPPINESS IS A PRACTICE, NOT A PERSONALITY TRAIT

Here are the daily habits that cultivate long-term happiness:

- gratitude journaling
- stable routines
- emotional boundaries
- choosing healthy relationships
- lowering chaos
- mindful breathing
- acts of compassion
- small joys
- movement
- getting sunlight
- saying "no" without guilt
- practicing presence
- celebrating small wins
- giving yourself permission to rest

Happiness thrives in structure, safety, and emotional clarity.

WORKSHEET: MY HAPPINESS BLUEPRINT

1. What currently brings me genuine joy?

(List people, experiences, sensory joys, habits.)

2. What drains me or dims my happiness?

3. What small daily habits naturally increase my happiness?

4. What belief about happiness did I inherit that no longer serves me?

5. When was the last time I felt a moment of pure happiness? What created it?

6. What environment do I thrive in emotionally?

7. What does "happiness" look like for the healed version of me?

JOURNAL PROMPTS FOR DEEP REFLECTION

1. What does happiness feel like in my body?
2. What version of me is afraid to be happy? Why?
3. What would it mean for my life if I allowed myself consistent joy?
4. What habits stop me from experiencing happiness?
5. What part of happiness do I not trust yet?
6. Who am I when I am truly happy?
7. How can I create a life that supports my joy instead of sabotaging it?

PRACTICES THAT IMMEDIATELY BOOST HAPPINESS (Evidence-Based)

1. The Three Good Things Practice

Each night list three things that went well today and why.

2. Micro-Joy Rituals

5-second joys:

fresh air

a favorite scent

stretching

music

sunlight

Small joy compounds over time.

3. The Gratitude Anchor

Name three things in the present moment you appreciate.

4. The Future Self Smile

Imagine your healed, happiest self.

What is she grateful you overcame?

5. Nervous System Reset Breathing

Inhale 4 seconds

Hold 2 seconds

Exhale 6 seconds

Calms anxiety and heightens emotional openness.

AFFIRMATIONS FOR HAPPINESS

- I allow myself to experience joy without fear.
- I deserve happiness I don't have to suffer for.
- Happiness is safe for me now.
- Small joys are still joys.
- I am learning how to let happiness stay.
- My life is making room for peace.
- I am worthy of a gentle, joyful, beautiful life.

DAY 76

THE RETURN OF DESIRE: RECLAIMING PLEASURE, PASSION, AND SELF-INTIMACY

Trauma dims your desires.

Healing reignites them.

Desire is not shameful.

Desire is not "too much."

Desire is not dangerous.

Desire is not sinful.

Desire is not a weakness.

Desire is a life force.

A spark.

A pulse.

A reminder that you are alive.

When you heal, your desires return:

- your desire for touch that feels safe
- your desire for connection

- your desire for creativity
- your desire for intimacy
- your desire for pleasure
- your desire for play
- your desire for beauty
- your desire for joy
- your desire for exploration
- your desire for self-expression

Your body begins trusting you again.

Your spirit begins awakening again.

Your senses begin sharpening again.

Your femininity rises again.

You are not "too much" for wanting pleasure—

you were simply deprived of it for too long.

Desire is not greed.

Desire is self-connection.

Quote:

"Your desire is holy. It means you survived."

Affirmation:

I honor my desires and allow pleasure back into my life.

WORKSHEET + SOMATIC HEALING

WORKSHEET: Reconnecting With My Desire

1. What desires have I suppressed?

2. What scared me about wanting more?

3. What does safe pleasure feel like?

4. What brings joy to my senses?

5. What do I want to explore about myself?

6. What desire am I reclaiming today?

Your Answers;

SOMATIC DESIRE PRACTICE: THE BODY REMEMBERS

- hand on chest
- other hand on stomach
- slow breaths
- ask:

"What does my body crave today?"

UNIVERSAL PRACTICE : "The Desire Awakening"

Light a candle or sit with soft light.

Whisper:

"I allow my desires to rise safely."

JOURNAL + AFFIRMATIONS

JOURNAL PROMPTS

1. What desires feel new to me?
2. What do I want to invite back into my body and spirit?
3. How do I define pleasure without shame?

AFFIRMATIONS

- My desires are valid.
- Pleasure belongs to me.
- I honor my sensuality with safety.
- I trust my body again.

DAY 77

THE ABUNDANT MINDSET: SHIFTING FROM SURVIVAL TO RECEIVING

After trauma, your mind lives in scarcity.

You learn to expect:

loss

abandonment

disappointment

broken promises

emotional instability

betrayal

struggle

pain

But healing teaches you abundance.

Abundance means:

believing you deserve good things

trusting that more is coming

expecting reciprocity

accepting love

allowing joy

receiving help

welcoming blessings

Abundance is not fantasy.

It is not delusion.

It is not arrogance.

Abundance is knowing:

"I do not have to suffer to receive."

"I am worthy of more."

"I do not have to beg life to bless me."

You shift from:

"I hope" to "I trust."

"I want" to "I deserve."

"I fear" to "I am prepared."

"I lack" to "I am aligned."

This is where your glow becomes magnetic.

Quote:

"*You are not asking for too much. You are remembering what you deserve.*"

Affirmation:

I am worthy of abundance in all forms.

WORKSHEET + MINDSET

WORKSHEET: My Abundant Life

1. Where do I still think in scarcity?

2. What abundance do I desire?

3. What blessing am I afraid to receive?

4. What limiting belief am I releasing?

5. What replaces that belief?

6. How can I welcome abundance today?

Your Answers;

MINDSET SHIFT: FROM LACK TO ALIGNMENT

Write your biggest fear.

Then write three truths that replace it.

UNIVERSAL PRACTICE: "Open Palm Receiving"

Sit with your palms open.

Inhale: "I welcome."

Exhale: "I receive."

JOURNAL + AFFIRMATIONS

JOURNAL PROMPTS

1. What abundance feels natural to me now?
2. What am I ready to receive without fear?
3. What belief about myself is changing?

AFFIRMATIONS

- Abundance flows to me effortlessly.
- I am worthy of more.
- My life expands beautifully.
- I am aligned with growth.

DAY 78

THE GLOW UP THROUGH HABITS: ELEVATING YOUR DAILY LIFE

Your glow up is not a moment.

It is a routine.

It is built through:

- consistent habits
- steady boundaries
- aligned choices
- daily peace
- self-discipline
- self-love
- emotional regulation
- rest and hydration
- clean spaces
- intentional style
- healthier sleep
- protecting your mornings
- protecting your nights

The glow up is not surgery, makeup, clothes, or trends...

it is the sum of everything you do behind the scenes.

Your habits are the backbone of your glow.

Every time you:

- drink water
- walk outside
- clean your space
- say no
- meditate
- stretch
- take vitamins
- wash your face
- rest
- move your body
- journal
- take responsibility
- stay consistent

... you glow stronger.

Quote:

"Small habits create the glow they swear is natural."

Affirmation:

My habits elevate me into the woman I am becoming.

WORKSHEET + ROUTINE

WORKSHEET: My Glow Up Habits

1. What habits improved my life the most?
2. What habits dim my glow?
3. What morning routine empowers me?
4. What night routine restores me?
5. What habit am I adding this week?
6. What habit am I releasing?

Your Answers;

ROUTINE BUILDER: 3 PILLARS OF THE GLOW UP

- Body care
- Mindset care
- Energy care

Add 1 habit to each.

UNIVERSAL PRACTICE : "The Glow Breath"

Over your heart:

"I rise into the woman I'm becoming."

JOURNAL + AFFIRMATIONS

JOURNAL PROMPTS

1. What habit changed my life?
2. What does my ideal day look like?
3. How can I create consistency with kindness?

AFFIRMATIONS

- My routines elevate me.
- My habits support my glow.
- I discipline myself with love.
- I rise daily in alignment.

DAY 79

THE FRIENDSHIP GLOW UP: CHOOSING COMMUNITY THAT MATCHES YOUR ENERGY

Healing changes your friendships.

You no longer tolerate:

jealousy

competition

backhanded compliments

draining conversations

low vibrational connections

trauma-bond friendships

people who only call when they need you

one-sided emotional labor

people who mock your boundaries

people who get offended when you grow

You now crave:

support

mutual care

consistency

celebration

peace

alignment

safe accountability

women who uplift you

women who inspire you

women who heal with you

friendships that feel like home

Friendship is not about proximity.

It is about emotional safety.

Healing elevates your standards for community.

Quote:

"*Your glow attracts women who see you—not women who fear your shine.*"

Affirmation:

I attract friendships that align with my healing and my glow.

WORKSHEET + INSIGHT

WORKSHEET: My Healed Friendships

1. What friendships nourish me?
2. What friendships drain me?
3. What do I need from my community?
4. What boundaries protect my energy?
5. What qualities define a safe friend?
6. What friendships am I releasing or redefining?

Your Answers;

INSIGHT: COMMUNITY HEALS TRAUMA

Healthy friendships regulate the nervous system,

strengthen emotional resilience,

and reinforce new patterns.

Healing is not done alone.

UNIVERSAL PRACTICE: "The Community Invite"

Say softly:

"I welcome aligned souls into my life."

JOURNAL + AFFIRMATIONS

JOURNAL PROMPTS

1. What does a safe friendship feel like?
2. How do I show up as a healed friend?
3. What friendships am I ready to nurture?

AFFIRMATIONS

- I attract aligned women.
- My friendships nourish me.
- I honor the community I build.
- My circle reflects my healing.

DAY 80

THE LIFE YOU'RE BUILDING: CREATING A FUTURE YOU'RE PROUD OF

This is the turning point.

You are no longer rebuilding from survival…

you are creating from vision.

Your future is no longer shaped by trauma.

It is shaped by intention.

You are building:

-
- a peaceful life
- a stable emotional world
- a healthy love story
- a nurturing home
- a regulated nervous system
- a confident identity
- a soft feminine glow

- a loving community
- a protected energy field
- a clear vision
- a healed mindset
- a future you once doubted

Your healing has shifted your destiny.

You don't dream the same.
You don't think the same.
You don't choose the same.
You don't settle for the same.

You are building a life that matches the woman you are becoming.

And that life is beautiful.

Quote:
"When you heal, your future expands."

Affirmation:
I am creating a future aligned with my highest self.

WORKSHEET + VISION WORK

WORKSHEET: Designing My Life

1. What does my ideal future look like?

2. What values define my next chapter?

3. What dreams feel possible again?

4. What do I want in love?

5. What do I want in career?

6. What do I want in lifestyle?

Your Answers;

VISION PRACTICE: 5-YEAR SELF LETTER

Write a letter from your future self to your present self describing:

- your life
- your home
- your peace
- your relationships
- your glow
- your career
- your joy

UNIVERSAL PRACTICE : "Future Alignment"

Close your eyes.

See the woman you'll be.

Whisper:

"She is me. I am her."

JOURNAL + AFFIRMATIONS

JOURNAL PROMPTS

1. What am I excited about in my future?
2. What steps align me with my next chapter?
3. What do I want my healed life to reflect?

AFFIRMATIONS

- My future is bright.
- My vision is clear.
- I walk toward alignment daily.
- My healed life is my masterpiece.

THE FINAL TRANSFORMATION

You've come so far.

Ninety days ago, you began this journey with uncertainty, fear, exhaustion, pain, hope, or a mixture of all of it. You entered this workbook carrying wounds you didn't ask for, memories you wish you could forget, and a life you desperately wanted to understand, escape, or rebuild.

And still you chose healing.

You showed up for yourself on days when your heart felt heavy.

You turned the page when you could have shut the book.

You told the truth when lying to yourself would have been easier.

You faced emotions you once avoided.

You honored your boundaries.

You reconnected with your body.

You rewrote your story.

You softened.

You strengthened.

You rose.

Now, you stand at the doorway of your final transformation.

These last ten days are not about survival.

They are not about understanding the past.

They are not about breaking patterns or naming wounds.

You've already done that work.

The final ten days are about becoming.

They are the closing chapter of your old self and the emergence of the woman who has always been waiting beneath the healing.

In these last ten days, you will:

1. Release the last emotional ties to your past

You'll let go of the final pieces… those lingering questions, attachments, memories, and hopes that try to keep you connected to a story that no longer deserves you.

2. Rewrite the narrative you once believed about yourself

You'll replace lies with truth, wounds with wisdom, and old scripts with new identity.

3. Protect your heart without building walls

You'll learn to love from a healed place. One that honors your intuition, boundaries, and self-worth

4. Step fully into your rebirth

You'll name the woman you've become and shape the life that supports her.

5. See yourself clearly for the first time

Not through trauma's eyes, but through truth, compassion, and pride.

6. Claim your worthiness without apology

You'll step into the life you deserve! One built on worth, not wounds.

7. Anchor yourself in peace

Peace will stop being something you chase and become something you carry.

8. Accept your value

Not superficially, but deeply, recognizing the rare, grounded, aligned woman you have become.

9. Align with your destiny

You'll step toward the path that was always meant for you, no longer distracted by anything beneath your standards.

10. Celebrate the fullness of your transformation

You will look back at the version of you who began this journey and realize she didn't just survive—she transformed.

These last ten days are sacred.

They are your closing ceremony.

Your confirmation.

Your full circle moment.

Your arrival.

You do not get to the end of this workbook as the woman you were.

You reach the end as the woman you were meant to be.

Welcome to your final transformation.

You earned it.

You embodied it.

You deserve every part of it.

And the best part?

This is only the beginning.

DAY 81

THE FINAL RELEASE: LETTING GO OF THE LAST PIECE OF THEM

There is always one last piece.

One memory.

One hope.

One fantasy.

One unanswered question.

One wound that lingers.

This piece is what keeps the past attached …

even after you've grown, healed, and risen.

Today is about releasing that piece.

You don't release because it didn't matter.

You release because it mattered too much.

Releasing doesn't erase your story …

it frees your future.

You're not letting go of love.

You're letting go of the weight.

You're letting go of the expectation.

You're letting go of the hurt.

You're letting go of the fear.

You're letting go of the invisible thread

that tied your survival to someone unhealed.

This is the release that honors your evolution.

Quote:

"Letting go is loving yourself louder."

Affirmation:

I release what no longer belongs to my future.

WORKSHEET + SOMATIC RESET

WORKSHEET: My Final Release

1. What piece of the past still follows me?
2. Why is it hard to release?
3. What truth do I need to accept?
4. What does my healed self gain from letting go?
5. What new space will open in my life?
6. Who am I without this attachment?

Your Answers;

SOMATIC RESET: THE SHOULDER DROP

Raise your shoulders.

Hold.

Release slowly.

Feel the weight fall off your body.

UNIVERSAL PRACTICE : "The Cord Release"

Close your eyes.

Picture the last attachment dissolving.

Whisper:

"I let it go."

JOURNAL + AFFIRMATIONS

JOURNAL PROMPTS

1. What am I freeing myself from today?
2. How does this release change my life?
3. What does freedom feel like in my body?

AFFIRMATIONS

- I am free.
- I am clear.
- I am open.
- I release with love.

DAY 82

THE REWRITING: CHANGING THE NARRATIVE YOU ONCE BELIEVED

You were told stories about yourself that were never true.

"You're too sensitive."

"You're too emotional."

"You're hard to love."

"You're dramatic."

"You're replaceable."

"You expect too much."

"You should be grateful."

"You need to calm down."

These were not truths ...

they were projections,

manipulations,

gaslighting,

and emotional abuse.

Healing means rewriting your narrative.

Your new truth is:

-
- You are emotionally intelligent, not "too sensitive."
- You are passionate, not "too much."
- You are lovable, not "hard to love."
- You are intuitive, not "dramatic."
- You are irreplaceable, not "easily replaced."
- You are deserving, not "difficult."
- You are aware, not "crazy."
- You are strong, not "broken."

You get to choose the story now.

Quote:

"Rewrite the narrative. You are the author now."

Affirmation:

I reclaim the truth of who I am.

WORKSHEET + MIND REFRAME

WORKSHEET: Rewriting My Story

1. What lies did I internalize?

2. Who gave me those lies?

3. What truth replaces each lie?

4. What proof do I have of that truth?

5. How does the new narrative feel?

6. What story am I choosing now?

Your Answers;

REFRAME EXERCISE: LIE TO TRUTH

Write the lie.

Cross it out.

Write the truth beneath it.

UNIVERSAL PRACTICE: "The Author's Declaration"

Hand over heart:

"I write my own story now."

JOURNAL + AFFIRMATIONS

JOURNAL PROMPTS

1. What lie hurt me the most?
2. What truth liberates me the most?
3. How do I embody my new story?

AFFIRMATIONS

- My truth is stronger than my past.
- I rewrite my story with power.
- I choose healing over history.
- I am the author of my life.

DAY 83

THE PROTECTED HEART: LOVING WITHOUT SELF-BETRAYAL

Love is not dangerous anymore.

Not when you love from a healed place.

Your heart is no longer exposed

like an open wound.

It is held, protected, and supported

by the woman you've become.

You learn to love without:

- overgiving
- losing yourself
- shrinking
- silencing your intuition
- ignoring red flags
- begging
- contorting yourself
- choosing potential
- accepting crumbs

Healed love is intentional.

Balanced.

Reciprocal.

Gentle.

Steady.

Safe.

You are not guarding your heart out of fear.

You are protecting it out of wisdom.

You are not avoiding love.

You are choosing healthy love.

Your heart is sacred.

Not everyone has access.

Quote:

"I protect my heart the way I protect my peace — with reverence."

Affirmation:

My heart is protected by my wisdom, not my fear.

WORKSHEET + PATTERN WORK

WORKSHEET: Protecting My Heart with Wisdom

1. What did love look like before healing?
2. What does love look like now?
3. What protects my heart?
4. What does my intuition tell me about connection?
5. What boundary safeguards my heart best?
6. What type of love do I welcome now?

Your Answers;

PATTERN WORK: LEARNED LOVE VS. HEALTHY LOVE

Write:

"What I was taught about love"

then

"What I now know to be true."

UNIVERSAL PRACTICE: "Heart Shield Activation"

Hands over heart.

Say:

"I protect my heart and honor who it loves."

JOURNAL + AFFIRMATIONS

JOURNAL PROMPTS

1. What kind of love does my heart deserve?
2. What love wounds have I healed?
3. How do I protect my heart with honor?

AFFIRMATIONS

- My heart is safe with me.
- I choose love with clarity.
- I deserve gentle connection.
- My heart is sacred.

DAY 84

THE SPIRIT OF REBIRTH: YOUR NEW LIFE AFTER SURVIVAL

Rebirth is not dramatic.

It is quiet.

It is steady.

It is sacred.

Rebirth is:

- new standards
- new boundaries
- new confidence
- new clarity
- new joy
- new identity
- new priorities
- new emotional world
- new ways of loving
- new ways of resting
- new ways of thinking

- new ways of being

Rebirth is not becoming someone new—

it is shedding who you were forced to be.

It is the moment you realize:

"I survived."

"I healed."

"I transformed."

"I am different now."

It's the breath you take in the morning and feel no dread.

It's the peace you feel when your phone vibrates and you don't panic.

It's the calm you feel when you set a boundary and don't apologize.

It's the joy that returns without permission.

You are not restarting.

You are rebirthing.

Quote:

"This is your second life. Honor it."

Affirmation:

I rise into my rebirth with peace and confidence.

WORKSHEET + IDENTITY

WORKSHEET: My Rebirth

1. What changes reflect my rebirth?
2. What am I no longer available for?
3. What aligns with my new life?
4. What emotion defines my rebirth?
5. What habits support my rebirth?
6. What do I want this new life to feel like?

Your Answers;

IDENTITY PRACTICE: THE REBIRTH LIST

Write:

"My new life looks like…"

Then list 10 truths.

UNIVERSAL PRACTICE : "The Rebirth Breath"

Deep inhale.

Soft exhale.

Say:

"I begin again."

JOURNAL + AFFIRMATIONS

JOURNAL PROMPTS

1. What part of me feels newly awakened?
2. What parts of my life feel reborn?
3. What will I protect in this new season?

AFFIRMATIONS

- I embrace my rebirth.
- My life is transforming beautifully.
- I protect the new version of me.
- I rise with purpose.

BONUS SECTION ii:

GRATITUDE & HUMILITY

How Healing, Truth, and Growth Work
Together for Your Good

Gratitude is not pretending it didn't hurt.

Humility is not minimizing what you survived.

This section is not about being thankful for pain.

It is about understanding how everything you lived through shaped who you became —

and choosing wisdom over resentment.

Gratitude and humility are not soft concepts.

They are the final signs of real healing.

WHAT GRATITUDE IS AND ISN'T

Gratitude is not:

- excusing abuse

- thanking people who harmed you

- bypassing anger

- forcing positivity

- denying grief

- spiritualizing trauma

- silencing your truth

Gratitude is:

- acknowledging growth

- honoring resilience

- recognizing clarity

- seeing lessons without glorifying pain

- understanding redirection

- appreciating discernment

- respecting your evolution

You do not have to be grateful for what broke you.

You can be grateful for who you became because you survived it.

HUMILITY: THE QUIET STRENGTH OF HEALING

Humility in healing means:

- accepting that you didn't know what you didn't know

- acknowledging where you stayed too long

- recognizing where survival blurred judgment

- admitting where pain shaped behavior

- allowing yourself to grow without shame

Humility is not self-blame.

It is self-honesty.

It says:

"I was wounded."

"I was human."

"I was learning."

"And now, I choose differently."

This is how cycles truly end.

THE PSYCHOLOGY: WHY GRATITUDE CHANGES THE BRAIN

Research shows:

- Gratitude strengthens the prefrontal cortex, improving emotional regulation

- Practicing gratitude lowers cortisol and reduces stress responses

- Gratitude increases serotonin and dopamine, improving mood stability

- Humility reduces defensiveness, increasing capacity for growth

- Gratitude helps the brain integrate trauma instead of relive it

Gratitude doesn't erase memory.

It reorganizes meaning.

Humility doesn't weaken you.

It frees you from ego-based pain.

HOW EVERYTHING WORKS TOGETHER FOR YOUR GOOD

This doesn't mean everything was good.

It means:

- what tried to break you sharpened your discernment
- what betrayed you taught you boundaries
- what confused you strengthened your intuition
- what you lost redirected your path
- what wounded you revealed your strength
- what didn't work saved you from what would've destroyed you

Some lessons come as gifts.

Others come as warnings.

Both serve you.

WHEN GRATITUDE BECOMES GROUNDED & NOT FORCED

Real gratitude sounds like:

"I see myself clearly now."

"I trust my judgment more."

"I don't beg for love anymore."

"I listen to my body."

"I walk away sooner."

"I value peace."

"I know who I am."

This is not spiritual language.

This is healed language.

WORKSHEET: INTEGRATING GRATITUDE WITHOUT DENIAL

Answer honestly. No rushing.

1. What did my pain teach me about myself that comfort never could?

2. What strengths emerged only because I survived hardship?

3. What patterns am I grateful to have outgrown?

4. What redirections saved me even if they hurt at the same time?

5. What do I appreciate about who I am now?

6. **What does humility allow me to release?**

JOURNAL PROMPTS

- Where has bitterness softened into wisdom?

- What do I see differently now that I couldn't see before?

- How has my pain deepened my compassion without weakening my boundaries?

- What am I grateful for in this season of my life?

- What does "working together for my good" look like in reality and not in theory?

A LETTER OF GRATITUDE TO MYSELF

Write a letter beginning with:

"Thank you for surviving what you didn't understand at the time…"

Thank the version of you who stayed.

Thank the version of you who left.

Thank the version of you who learned.

Thank the version of you who healed.

This is humility in action.

AFFIRMATIONS: GRATITUDE WITH TRUTH

- I am grateful for my growth, not the harm.
- I honor the lessons without glorifying the pain.
- I release resentment and keep wisdom.
- Everything I lived through sharpened my discernment.
- I walk forward with humility, not shame.
- I trust that my life is unfolding with purpose.
- I am at peace with who I am becoming.

CLOSING TRUTH

Gratitude is not the absence of anger.

Humility is not the absence of confidence.

Together, they are the presence of wisdom.

And wisdom is how healing becomes legacy.

DAY 85

THE WOMAN IN THE MIRROR: SEEING YOURSELF WITH FULL TRUTH

Look at yourself.

Really look.

You see:

- the survivor
- the healer
- the soft one
- the strong one
- the intuitive one
- the wise one
- the loving one
- the glowing one
- the reborn one

You see a woman who lived through storms

she never deserved

and still chose compassion.

Still chose love.

Still chose healing.

Still chose herself.

You see a woman who carried more than she should have and still stands.

You see a woman you can be proud of.

This woman is not broken.

She is not weak.

She is not unworthy.

She is a masterpiece built from truth.

Quote:

"You are the woman you once prayed to become."

Affirmation:

I see myself clearly, and I am proud.

WORKSHEET + REFLECTION

WORKSHEET: Seeing My Truth

1. What do I see when I look at myself now?
2. What has changed within me?
3. What strengths do I now recognize?
4. What beauty do I now acknowledge?
5. What truth about myself is undeniable?
6. What do I love about who I am?

Your Answers;

REFLECTION PRACTICE: MIRROR TRUTH

Stand in front of a mirror.

Say three things you admire about yourself.

UNIVERSAL PRACTICE : "The Mirror Blessing"

Hand on chest:

"I honor the woman I see."

JOURNAL + AFFIRMATIONS

JOURNAL PROMPTS

1. Who am I today compared to Day 1?
2. What part of myself do I appreciate most?
3. How has my self-image healed?

AFFIRMATIONS

- I see myself with love.
- My reflection is my strength.
- I am proud of my growth.
- I honor my evolution.

DAY 86

THE LIFE YOU DESERVE: WORTHINESS WITHOUT LIMITS

You are worthy of:

- peace
- love
- joy
- stability
- respect
- softness
- consistent affection
- devotion
- commitment
- safety
- comfort
- reciprocity
- abundance
- beauty
- expansion

Not because you earned it.

Not because you suffered.

Not because you healed.

Not because you were perfect.

You are worthy because you exist.

You are worthy of a life that requires no suffering to receive.

You don't have to prove your worth.

You don't have to beg for worth.

You don't have to hustle for worth.

You don't have to audition for worth.

You are worth.

Quote:

"Your worthiness is unconditional."

Affirmation:

I deserve a life filled with love, peace, and abundance.

WORKSHEET + WORTHINESS WORK

WORKSHEET: What I Deserve

1. What do I believe I deserve now?
2. What did I used to settle for?
3. What does worthiness feel like?
4. What am I ready to receive without fear?
5. What blessing feels aligned?
6. What life am I stepping into?

WORTHINESS PRACTICE: "I DESERVE" STATEMENTS

Write 10 sentences beginning with:

"I deserve…"

Your Answers;

UNIVERSAL PRACTICE: "The Worth Breath"

Inhale: "I deserve."

Exhale: "I receive."

JOURNAL + AFFIRMATIONS

JOURNAL PROMPTS

1. What part of my worth was once hidden?
2. How do I honor my worth daily?
3. What does a worthy life feel like to me?

AFFIRMATIONS

- I am worthy.
- I accept all aligned blessings.
- I honor my divine worth.
- I welcome abundance.

THE DAY 87

THE PEACE PROTECTOR: LIVING WITH INTENTIONAL CALM

Peace is your superpower now.

Not because life is perfect,

but because you are different.

Peace is not the absence of problems.

Peace is the presence of emotional maturity.

Peace looks like:

- not responding
- staying quiet
- choosing distance
- protecting your mornings
- blocking chaos
- not entertaining disrespect
- walking away
- breathing before reacting

- knowing what triggers you
- choosing alignment over impulse

Peace is a lifestyle.

It is the discipline of choosing yourself

over drama, ego, chaos, and old patterns.

Quote:

"*My peace is my new identity.*"

Affirmation:

Peace is my home and I protect it fiercely.

WORKSHEET + ROUTINE

WORKSHEET: Protecting My Peace

1. What disturbs my peace the most?
2. What helps me regulate quickly?
3. What reactions am I releasing?
4. What habits maintain my calm?
5. What boundaries protect my tranquility?
6. What does peace mean for me now?

Your Answers;

ROUTINE: PEACE PROTOCOL

When triggered, ask:

1. "Is this mine?"
2. "Does this matter?"
3. "Is this aligned?"

UNIVERSAL PRACTICE : "The Peace Shield"

Close your eyes.

Say:

"Peace surrounds me. Peace protects me."

JOURNAL + AFFIRMATIONS

JOURNAL PROMPTS

1. What does peace feel like in my body?
2. When did I choose peace over reaction?
3. How will I protect my peace moving forward?

AFFIRMATIONS

- Peace is my grounding.
- I walk in calm strength.
- My reactions are intentional.
- My peace is sacred.

DAY 88

THE HIGH-VALUE SELF: RECOGNIZING YOUR POWER, PRESENCE, & IMPACT

High value is not about money, looks, or status.

It is about emotional quality.

A high-value woman is:

- self-aware
- emotionally regulated
- deeply intuitive
- clear on her boundaries
- selective
- rare
- aligned
- wise
- soft and strong
- disciplined
- intentional
- peaceful
- confident

- grounded

You have become her through healing.

High value is your energy,

your wisdom,

your peace,

your standards,

your glow,

your intuition,

your discernment,

your softness,

your strength.

You are no longer intimidated by being rare.

You finally accept that you are the blessing.

Quote:
"Your value is undeniable. Your presence is powerful."

Affirmation:
I am a high-value woman with rare energy.

WORKSHEET + IDENTITY

WORKSHEET: My High-Value Identity

1. What qualities make me high-value?
2. What boundaries uphold my value?
3. What habits reflect my rarity?
4. What behaviors diminish my value?
5. What environments honor my worth?
6. How do I carry myself as a high-value woman?

Your Answers;

IDENTITY PRACTICE: CLAIM YOUR VALUE

Say confidently:

"I am the prize."

UNIVERSAL PRACTICE: "The Crown Touch"

Gently touch the top of your head.

Whisper:

"I carry myself with royalty."

JOURNAL + AFFIRMATIONS

JOURNAL PROMPTS

1. When did I first realize my value?
2. What standards reflect my worth?
3. How do I embody my rarity daily?

AFFIRMATIONS

- I am rare.
- I am valuable.
- My presence shifts rooms.
- I carry myself with grace and power.

DAY 89

THE DESTINY ALIGNMENT: WALKING THE PATH YOU WERE MEANT FOR

Your destiny was never destroyed by what you survived.

It was shaped by it.

Every heartbreak refined your clarity.

Every betrayal sharpened your intuition.

Every ending redirected your path.

Every wound expanded your capacity.

Every lesson clarified your standards.

Every trigger strengthened your resilience.

You are not behind —

you are aligned.

Destiny alignment means:

- you stop settling
- you stop forcing
- you stop chasing

- you stop doubting
- you stop shrinking
- you stop apologizing

You start:

- listening
- trusting
- moving in silence
- protecting your calling
- following your intuition
- choosing aligned environments
- stepping into purpose

Your destiny is not ahead of you.

It is within you.

Quote:

"What is meant for you cannot be lost — only delayed until you heal enough to receive it."

Affirmation:

I walk in alignment with my destiny.

WORKSHEET + PURPOSE WORK

WORKSHEET: Aligning My Destiny

1. What is calling me in this season?
2. What no longer aligns with my path?
3. What purpose am I stepping into?
4. What talents am I reclaiming?
5. What does alignment feel like?
6. What step brings me closer to my destiny?

Your Answers;

PURPOSE PRACTICE: DESTINY STATEMENT

Write a sentence beginning with:

"I am meant for..."

UNIVERSAL PRACTICE : "The Purpose Anchor"

Hand on heart.

Whisper:

"Guide me where I am meant to go."

JOURNAL + AFFIRMATIONS

JOURNAL PROMPTS

1. What path feels most aligned right now?
2. What dream refuses to die?
3. What does my destiny look like?

AFFIRMATIONS

- I am aligned.
- My destiny unfolds gracefully.
- I walk with purpose.
- I trust my path.

DAY 90

THE FULL CIRCLE: CELEBRATING THE WOMAN YOU HAVE BECOME

This is Day Ninety.

You made it.

You didn't just read a workbook.

You transformed your life.

Look at you.

You:

- healed
- grew
- shed
- released
- rebirthed
- glowed
- rose
- aligned

- protected
- discerned
- loved
- softened
- strengthened
- returned

You did not quit.

You did not fold.

You did not abandon yourself.

You became the woman your past self needed.

You became the woman your future self deserves.

You became the healed, whole, glowing, powerful you.

This is your full circle moment.

You are no longer surviving.

You are living.

You are thriving.

You are free.

Quote:

"I am the evidence that healing works."

Affirmation:

I honor my transformation and celebrate who I have become.

WORKSHEET + REFLECTION

WORKSHEET: My Transformation

1. What changed the most in these 90 days?
2. What part of my healing surprised me?
3. What wound did I finally close?
4. What new identity did I embody?
5. What blessing did healing make room for?
6. What promise will I make to myself moving forward?

Your Answers;

REFLECTION PRACTICE: LETTER TO SELF

Write a letter to yourself from Day 90

to your self on Day 1.

Tell her everything she overcame.

UNIVERSAL PRACTICE : "The Completion Breath"

Hand on heart.

Deep breath.

Say:

"Thank you for choosing me."

JOURNAL + AFFIRMATIONS

JOURNAL PROMPTS

1. Who am I now?
2. What does healed me feel like?
3. What new chapter am I ready to begin?

AFFIRMATIONS

- I am whole.
- I am transformed.
- I am powerful.
- I am free.

✓ PHASE THREE COMPLETE

ACKNOWLEDGMENTS

To every survivor who has ever felt unseen:

Thank you for your courage. Thank you for your voice. Thank you for your existence.

You are the reason this book lives.

To the domestic violence community

 the women, children, advocates, counselors, and generational cycle breakers ...

thank you for your strength, your stories, and your relentless fight for safety and healing.

To every woman who ever questioned her worth, her sanity, her voice, or her strength:

I see you. This book is your mirror.

To my supporters, my community, and every person who has poured love into me during my own rebuilding journey. Your presence helped shape this work.

And to God the source of my resilience, the hand that carried me through trauma, the breath behind my purpose, and the light that guided every word in these pages — thank you.

This book is bigger than me.

It is for all of us.

Why This Workbook Exists

This workbook was created for the person who is tired of hurting, tired of surviving, tired of choosing everyone else first, and ready...finally ...to choose herself.

It is for the woman who has walked through quiet storms, emotional violence, manipulation, abandonment, trauma bonds, and the kind of heartbreak that doesn't just break your heart... it breaks your identity.

I wrote this for the woman who needs a safe place to fall apart and rebuild again.

I wrote this for the woman who wants to understand what happened to her,

why she stayed,

why she broke,

why she rose,

and how she can become whole.

This is not a book of theories.

It is a book of truth that is lived truth, felt truth, scar truth, survivor truth.

These pages are structured to walk you through:

- awakening your awareness
- understanding trauma bonds
- breaking generational patterns
- naming inner wounds

- reclaiming boundaries
- returning to your body
- healing your nervous system
- rebuilding your identity
- protecting your peace
- glowing from within

and stepping into the person you were always meant to be.

This workbook will challenge you, soften you, stretch you, and return you to yourself.

I wrote this with reverence, intention, and love because every woman deserves a path back home to herself.

~Tiffany

ABOUT THE AUTHOR

Tiffany A. Morgan

Tiffany A. Morgan is a survivor, advocate, storyteller, and vessel of truth.

Born in Brooklyn and raised in Louisiana, Tiffany has transformed her own lived experiences into empowerment for women navigating trauma, domestic violence, toxic relationships, and the journey back to themselves.

She is a community activist, an outspoken voice for survivors, and an actress who brings raw emotion and authenticity to both stage and film. Her work is rooted in compassion, lived understanding, and a fierce dedication to healing.

Through her writing, Tiffany creates safe spaces for women to feel seen.

She teaches emotional awareness, boundaries, self-love, and resilience with honesty and depth. Her mission is simple: to help women remember who they are beneath the pain, and guide them back to the version of themselves they were always meant to become.

Not Easily Broken: 90 Days of Raw Healing is her most intimate and transformative work, a testimony of survival, identity, and the power of rising again.

Here are some coparenting resources that are also listed on the website:

RESOURCES & REFERENCES

This workbook is grounded in trauma research, emotional psychology, attachment theory, behavioral science, family systems, and survivor-centered healing.

The following works and authors—including Black mental health professionals, scholars, and healers—provide foundational insight into the themes explored throughout this book.

I. Trauma, Healing, and Nervous System Regulation

Bessel van der Kolk

The Body Keeps the Score

Somatic trauma, body memory, emotional regulation.

Peter Levine

Waking the Tiger: Healing Trauma

Somatic experiencing and nervous system release.

Stephen Porges

The Polyvagal Theory

Safety, threat response, nervous system regulation.

Judith Herman

Trauma and Recovery

Landmark work on relational trauma and healing.

Tara Brach

Radical Acceptance

Mindfulness, compassion, emotional grounding.

II. Black Mental Health Experts, Healers, and Scholars

Black Psychologists, Therapists, and Trauma Educators

Dr. Thema Bryant

Homecoming: Overcome Fear and Trauma to Reclaim Your Whole Authentic Self

Trauma recovery, cultural identity, soul healing, embodied resilience.

Dr. Joy Harden Bradford

Creator of Therapy for Black Girls

Podcast + mental health education for Black women.

Nedra Glover Tawwab

Set Boundaries, Find Peace and Drama Free

Boundaries, family dysfunction, emotional wellness.

Dr. Mariel Buqué

Break the Cycle

Intergenerational trauma, family healing, nervous system repair.

Dr. Stacey Patton

Spare the Kids: Why Whupping Children Won't Save Black America

Black childhood trauma, discipline, historical context.

Dr. Jennifer Mullan

Decolonizing Therapy

Healing trauma through cultural liberation and emotional reclamation.

Black Authors Exploring Trauma, Identity, and Emotional Recovery

bell hooks

All About Love

Love, healing childhood wounds, emotional honesty.

Iyanla Vanzant

Acts of Faith and Yesterday, I Cried

Spiritual healing, self-awareness, generational trauma.

Yaba Blay

One Drop

Identity, belonging, cultural narratives.

Brittney Cooper

Eloquent Rage

Black womanhood, emotional empowerment, truth-telling.

Tarana Burke

Unbound: My Story of Liberation and the Birth of the Me Too Movement

Sexual trauma, survivorhood, empowerment.

Kiese Laymon

Heavy

Memoir about trauma, body memory, family wounds.

III. Attachment Theory and Emotional Patterns

John Bowlby

Attachment and Loss

Hazan, C. & Shaver, P. (1987)

"Romantic love conceptualized as an attachment process."

Janina Fisher

Healing the Fragmented Selves of Trauma Survivors

IV. Trauma Bonds, Manipulation, and Interpersonal Abuse

Patrick Carnes
The Betrayal Bond

Susan Forward
Emotional Blackmail

Nina W. Brown
Children of the Self-Absorbed

Alice Miller
The Drama of the Gifted Child

V. Narcissism, Family Systems, and Emotional Neglect

Salvador Minuchin
Families and Family Therapy

Susan Forward
Toxic Parents

Lindsay C. Gibson
Adult Children of Emotionally Immature Parents

VI. Neuroscience of Bonding and Emotional Memory

Kosfeld, M., et al. (2005)
"Oxytocin increases trust in humans."
Nature, 435, 673–676.

Schultz, W. (2012)
"Dopamine reward prediction-error signalling."
Current Opinion in Neurobiology, 22(2), 201–207.

McGaugh, J. L. (2000)

"Memory — a century of consolidation."

Science, 287(5451), 248–251.

VII. Accountability, Behavioral Growth, and Self-Development

James Clear

Atomic Habits

Gabor Maté

When the Body Says No

Daniel Goleman

Emotional Intelligence

VIII. Domestic Violence Support and Crisis Resources

If you are in danger or feel unsafe, use the following resources:

National Domestic Violence Hotline (U.S.)

1-800-799-7233

Text "START" to 88788

www.thehotline.org

National Sexual Assault Hotline (RAINN)

1-800-656-4673

www.rainn.org

National Suicide & Crisis Lifeline

Call or text 988

Love Is Respect (Teens & Young Adults)

1-866-331-9474

www.loveisrespect.org

For global resources:

www.hotpeachpages.net

(Directory of international crisis centers)

IX. Suggested Reading for Deeper Reflection

The Body Is Not an Apology — Sonya Renee Taylor

Belonging — Toko-pa Turner

What Happened to You? — Bruce Perry & Oprah Winfrey

The Mountain Is You — Brianna Wiest

The Gift of Fear — Gavin de Becker

Where the Light Enters — Jill Biden

Women Who Love Too Much — Robin Norwood

Adult Children of Emotionally Immature Parents — Lindsay Gibson

Author's Note on Sources

This workbook is based on the author's interpretations of trauma-informed education, emotional development, boundaries, attachment theory, survivor research, and lived experience.

The authors and works listed above represent the educational and cultural foundations that inform this healing framework.

www.ingramcontent.com/pod-product-compliance
Lightning Source LLC
Chambersburg PA
CBHW051120160426
43195CB00014B/2275